A Small Goodbye at Dawn

Gill Lambert

ISBN: 978-1-913122-28-7

Cover image: 'Chrysalis' by Caroline Brown
                https://www.carolinebrownartist.com/

Cover design: Mike Farren

Editing: Mark Connors

Typesetting: Mike Farren

Acknowledgements

Many thanks to editors and publishers of magazines, anthologies and websites where some of these poems, or earlier versions, first appeared: *Dreich*; *Ink Sweat and Tears*; *Blue Nib*; *Black Light Engine Room*; *International Times*; *Reel Bradford* (Yaffle Press); *Bloody Amazing* (Beautiful Dragons/Yaffle Press); *The View from Olympia* (Half Moon Books); *An Insubstantial Universe* (Yaffle Press); *Distance and Home* (Leeds Trinity University, Word Space and Indigo Dreams Publishing 2021).

'Medusa's Walk of Shame' was included in Joe Williams' radio show *Sound and Vision* for Chapel fm's *Writing on Air* festival, 2021.

Special thanks go to these people: Mike Farren for his expert and speedy typesetting, Holly Bars, Hilary Robinson, Rachel Davies, Matt Nicholson, Edwin Stockdale, Rebecca Bilkau, Clare Shaw, Kim Moore, Jennifer. A. McGowan, Joe Williams, Lucy Heuschen, Zelda Chappel.

And to Mark Connors for content editing and making my life better, in all things.

The participants of all my workshops who continue to inspire my own writing with theirs.

For the use of her wonderful painting 'Chrysalis', I am indebted to Caroline Brown:

https://www.carolinebrownartist.com/

Finally, to Anne Boleyn for speaking her words in my ear and helping me tell other women's, and my own, story through hers.

Contents:

for Mark, always

Namak

At twelve, she makes a home.
They give her salt, *for flavour*,
and she remembers its importance;
a simple version of 'King Lear', Cordelia,
who told her father, not *nothing*,
but that she loved him more than salt.

Red is lifted from white with half a cup.
Her sterile shame; a line of pale pink gussets,
lost-tooth wound made clean
with just one mouthful. In her garden
slugs dissolve, unwanted. Dead.

The Devil's on her left; she does not fear him,
though she throws spilled salt over her shoulder,
whispers it, like prayer, into cooking water.
She remembers again, Cordelia – her *nothing*
but how she loved her father.

How *her* father loved *her*,
gave her away, like salt.

Lemon

I hardly remember them now.
Just enough to miss them, their sweet
over-spill into bite. I used to bleach
my freckles, so I fit in

with white-faced girls, their pale hair
in long curtains. But the juice
was never sufficient and I'm old now;
my skin all open pores, wax-drab.

In the mornings I pick dark hairs
from my pillow, wonder
where they came from. My own face
looks back at me from the mirror.

I still long for the shine,
the tight taste of bitterness.

Medusa's walk of shame

The rain has wet the streets. A burger wrapper dancing up the middle of the road is fixed by drizzle to the railings of a church. Their hangovers beat time to the rap from a taxi. A pack of them, hungry for their Sunday Full English. They whisper side-long, but they can't look at her, it's all they can do to keep their heads up. They lift their eyes from their hair-of-the-dog pints, she's just one glance from Costa to the bus-stop and there's safety-glass between them so even if she looks, she'll only see herself reflected back. She's every girl they've ever known; all their mothers, wives, daughters. Anybody's sister.

Take a name

any name, it won't matter, they're all dead.
Her – died in 1874 at the age of 40.
Spinster, Mary Jenkins. She'll do.
Imagine her: early life, mother, father,
siblings, where she went to school.

The colour of her eyes. The squint she had.
Her hair tied up, in rags for Sunday chapel.
Loose, the one time a man smoothed
over it with his palm, his hand calloused
from work, his breath sticky and sour
from three hours at the public house.

And our Mary, in the lane. Feeding hens,
picking buttercups? Gathering wood
for the fire about to go out and her mother
in bed with a fever she will not get over.
Her dad asleep in his chair, beer
from the same barrel in his belly
as the man about to stoke Mary's hair.

Mary lets him. The first bit of affection
she's had since her sister went into service.
Jenny, all blonde curls and bosoms,
at that moment in the arms of a butler
who will not do the honourable thing
when Jen ends up pregnant and about
to be out on her ear. But that's Jenny,
we are concerned with her sister

Mary. She lets the man kiss her, his hand
(the same one that two minutes earlier
was touching her locks) gathers
a handful of petticoat, pulls it up.
Mary gasps, tries to scream but
it's Sunday there's no one to hear.

The man goes home falls asleep
in his chair, wakes at nine, sober
to forget about Mary but goes to bed
for the first sex he's had with his wife
since the twins. The baby he puts in her
belly is their last one. Grows up cherished.

Mary's child is born still. That's after
she's sent to the workhouse, her Mam dead,
and no point in her good-for-nowt father.
She stays there the rest of her life, dies at 40.
Well, you know that already. Poor Mary.

Sparrow

for Olga Korbut

She used to be a bird;
they kept her tiny,
just how they liked her.

They felt her muscles,
poked her bones under her feathers,
watched for development.

She pulled the crowds,
bent over backwards,
even when it hurt her.

Mistakes were not encouraged,
nothing less than flawless.
She smiled, kept her chin up.

She lost the knack of flying.
Gave way to perfect tens
and headed West.

These days she keeps her head down,
locks the door against Recovery,
agents of the government.

Charlotte

I think you spoke my language;
blunt words cut off. The moors
in every syllable, each vowel
breathless from fresh air walks,
blushing your cheeks, pulling
at your coat.

Your small quiet world, not so far
away from mine, left you silent
when you tried to speak.
Gave back the words you took,
though it had more from you:
brother, sisters, child.

Cherry Pink and Apple Blossom White
for Vera

I think of you at twelve,
your hair in plaits, home-knit Aran,
shy National Health smile.
Ten years after the end of the war,
'normality' still a word you looked for
among the rationing, the Singer
sewing machine belting out
new from old.

I often imagine I was there
at the beginning, synchronising
with your mother and your sisters.
Every four weeks, all seven of us in time.

Myth

She'd lived on an island long enough to know the feeling of being at the edge, how the sway of it gave her vertigo, how the sea rose up. When she pulled him out of the water she felt the weight of being submerged, he wrapped himself round her till they both felt they were drowning. Though she was no Calypso, she'd wanted to save him. Not in the usual way; she never meant to become some myth-maker, but original thought is not an everyday occurrence and he'd been easy enough to keep alive. The heads of a Hydra grow back, like lies and language, cut one off, one word dies, there's another in its place.

Ghosts and fairies

(Fairy Tale: A True Story – Charles Sturridge, 1997)

She waits for the post, though she knows it won't come.
She's heard all she is going to.

Waits, with a mouthful of pins,
letting down the hem on my white pinafore.

I want to tell her *spit them out Mother*, but I am barefoot
and careful, standing perfectly still.

Your name is a nail, washed down with beck-silt
and the weeds take root.

It will not be spoken; I swallow it,
walk on tip-toes so she thinks I have grown.

My sorrow is a game made from paper,
tucked into crannies in loose brickwork.

And I know you belonged here once,
born on a black night halfway through the year,

summer a dull quiet. You stayed till the winter
and war was a whisper.

Fathers and brothers are ghosts and fairies. Mothers
and daughters stay silent

and weeds tangle inside me.
I don't know any more which is real.

I can't say your name;
it may as well be the King of the fairies.

So I cut paper, fold it, hide it in roof tiles.
Long after the last flame

ghosts and fairies are one and the same.
I can't tell any more.

Fallen

And afterwards the snow fell.
It muffled our footsteps from his house
to mine, our breath rising in speech bubbles,
although we had nothing left to say.
And my mother, pacing at the lateness,
watching from an upstairs window,
heard me brush myself down in our hall
as he walked away for the first time.
And it carried on falling, layer on layer
covering up what I'd done
in the space of an evening. When I'd gone
from one thing to another without speaking.
And in the morning I woke and looked out
on a world that had hidden its sins.

Lex Caesarea

Unbury me.
Lay my bones
out, click them
back into place.
A faithful shroud
will cover my scars
which speak of my
endurance, tell that I
was brave. Feel the hard
raised ridge of skin, unpick
its scabs, unravel it. Bring her
body back to me, the baby ripped
from mine to be the separate soul
they said she had to be. See her
come to life, re-bury her in me,
repair the clumsy slash and
watch the wound which
marks me *Mother*
fade to a
silver
smile.

Breakwater

It stops the tide,
the sea's pernicious energy.
Makes a safe harbour.

You are on your back.
They tell you after
breaking the water
the waves will increase
in intensity. You wait.

The sea is stopped
by structures which absorb
its power.

You feel the waves.
Hear them coming in your head
before they rise like surf
and you rise with them, your body
hit by oxytocin and saline.
But they will not be absorbed.

Rubble mound breakwaters
consist of piles of stones
which act as an armour layer
protecting the core from wave attack.

Your armour is peeled back.
All the words they taught you
over months and weeks.
Remember to breathe.
You try, but it's all you can do
to face each wave. You hold
your breath instead.

A row of 4 front side slabs
made to oscillate under the effect
of the incident wave, creates waves
in phase opposition to the incident
wave downstream from the slabs.

Now, they come on top of each other.
Wave on wave. You no longer know
when one ends and another begins.
You are out there, on your own.
Your friends have no idea where you are.
Your husband can't reach you. Even those
who are here to save you don't bring you
back from each brink. Someone
calls your name, but you can't answer.

One summer

Six weeks into a dry spell, parched gardens
forced brittle stubble into our bare legs.

We rode no-handed down the Big Hill
through cat-piss snickets, dog shit baking,

made dens under Leylandii in powdered earth,
watched the hours slide through lilac.

Hand-sewn sundresses jazzed up with ric-rac,
worn vest-less, rubbed the buds of our new womanhood.

We played Top Trumps, memorised capacities of cars
we'd never own with boys we'd never marry,

though we went with them into stifling tents
which stayed up all summer;

progressed from closed-mouth kissing by September.
And our mothers reclined on sun-loungers,

sipped coffee in the mornings after chores.
Oiled and polished, they popped Valium with Cuba Libre

that reminded them of Spanish package holidays
and made them bold enough to contemplate their freedom.

Half-term, 1978

I forget why we were there on our own,
ignoring public information films
about strangers, playing near railways.
I had no words then, to tell you;
you only mumbled something about Man U,
pushed your sleeves up;
your brother said it was cool.

You were so close I smelt the outside on you,
not soap and shampoo, like at school,
but wood-smoke, Juicy Fruit.
I felt your dry-lipped kiss,
the thin hum through my body
when a train passed.

Crownless

These words I've learned
are nothing new.
Every woman I have known
has learned the same ones.
You think they're mine,
from a new place,
a new mouth,
when all I've done
is tell you
what you already know.

Le temps viendra

She writes the words before she is what she'll become,
between coloured pages, in her book of hours.
The words are not a lie, though it is years until
she'll know the truth of them. Her name a careful script,
next to signatures of those who will betray her.

For now she is Anne. Sister. Daughter. Scholar.
Yet to be lover, mother. She makes
her pen form words in a strange tongue, speaks
its translation: *the time will come*. A prophecy,
a spell from the quill of a girl whose sight
is long. Or the ambitious dream
of a child with desires she can't fulfil.

These words, passed hand to hand down lines of kin
will prove her legacy, and shape her sin.

Who I am

Call me witch, say
I've cast spells. A man
taken in by one word is undone.

Point at me, sailing
on Thames tide from Greenwich
to Westminster Abbey. *Nan Bullen.*

Call me witch, stare.
Whisper your hex on the child
you all know is there. Shout *whore,*

goggle-eyed, plotter and *tease.*
Common-stewed. Call me *Boleyn.*
Call me *Anne.* Soon, you will all call me *Queen.*

Uncovered

This winter her head feels the cold.
A nagging chill. Pulled from her bed
on the mornings when she'd rather sleep.
A dread she remembers from childhood
is a stone in her gut.

The cold keeps her quiet.
Fastens her lips, chaps them with frost.
She's silent for fear she'll be found out.
Tells lies, pretends she can't speak.

She wants to be fearless; face the day
without feeling the ache. The lightness
of an earlier sunrise is memory now.
Shifts of darkness clock in and clock out.
She feels her way.

Oak

She spread herself wide. Searched,
dark-eyed for the sun through my branches.
Tilted her head back and sighed, gathered
fistfuls of fabric, pulled up her skirts.

He opened his hand like a tree,
flexed his fingers, pushed roots
into moist fertility, heard his heart
beat inside her, made promises.

I am gone. A hundred years since
they cut me down whole, used me
for pulpits and pews, a New World.
Now I am everywhere.

Yule

I know before he gets up from the bed,
wipes himself clean with a linen cloth.
I know from the way my thickening womb
grows warm; safe harbour for the royal seed.
I know he loves me, he has waited for this
without ire or bile, kissed my private places
but never took me, as was his right.
I know I please him. His face tells me this.
I know he will rise and dress, go to his men,
ride dangerously fast and hard, drink and dance,
celebrate this feast of light in winter
and give thanks to the God we have both shamed.
I will lie for a while, my secret budding,
and flowering into my saviour.
I know this comfort cannot last forever.
I know I'm but a vessel for his son.

Peach

Gold to blush,
I am velvet.
He waits till just before
my flesh turns sour, falls,
reveals the stone beneath.

He rips each layer with his teeth
and I can feel him tasting me,
licking round the edges.
He doesn't waste a drop.

Once I couldn't wait for this;
I had him where he has me.
Now it's started,
I cannot let it stop.

He's unpeeling me,
stripping me of skin.
I can only watch
all that promise,
all my power,
running down his chin.

Hidden

I'll tell them when I feel him move. Though my courses are as familiar to them as their own, they will know I have not bled. I want him for myself, before bog-eyed old men poke at me and wise women incant their premonitions. I want to stare from windows at blond boys playing with their friends in stable yards. Solid young men skip their lessons to laze in the sun. There is nothing to be done but wait, roll words round in my mouth, stones from cherries hidden inside my cheek. Soon, I will spit them out, watch them bloom, or dry and fade in the barren earth.

For hope

You have made a shawl of lace for this
new life. Too late. A sea is pulling
you away. This pain is waves; forward,
shrinking back.

A crescent moon half-smile fools them
and they leave you. Your blood is loud.
Last time it caved you in, reduced you.
You shift, become more liquid.

A soft heartbeat pesters you awake.
You sense lavender for distrust
and there are many here
who'd want you dead – sage for esteem.
Almond at the gateway of birth.

Heir

In my dream she's still inside me,
small fists balled against her womb-cell.
Impatient knuckles
nudging me from sleep.

When I wake it's to an empty room.
The secret of my girl-child
outside its walls.

Stain

It's here again, spreading
from middle to edges.
An end to it.

And the ache in my thighs;
pricking nipples.

I sit in blood and milk.
Five, six minutes,
before I tell.

Michaelmas

The year slips into autumn. He spends his evenings
drifting. He's with me, though he's long since left me.
While sunlit hours burn the last heat of the days,
I watch him as he turns away. I sit in shadow,
wait, while others chronicle my fall.

When candlelight is all there is, when wood smoke
stings, I will not cry. At the end I will remember
summer, its sweetness on my lips. When
every flower's dried to nothing, the bees
all dead and honey left is given to another.

The light's already fading. When the winter's here,
the dark pervading every corner of this place,
there will be nothing left to do but sleep.
I stitch my name to cloth so that my son,
should he ever come, will know his mother.

Dyed

I'm making a cap from fine red yarn.
The shade of his heritage, Tudor rose.
My needles are thin-slick. They move
as he shifts, remind me my days are
almost done. He won't come;
two more months till I'm able to cry.
I'm a fly cast in amber, the prettiest
feather. Sharp-snared bait.

My fingers are numb from needle ends.
Lace makes me ache, sitting still,
knitting this crown for a prince
come to term. Grubby grey fleece
made crimson with basil wood,
madder and cinnabar seething
in limewater. Rubbed on stone,
steeped in verdigris. Dragon's blood.

Unborn

Another serpent slips from me,
swims in water,
melts into the red.

I have a belly full,
writhing inside me.
Too small for arms and legs;
they are all face, all head.

Afterwards

they huddled in corners, whispered her loss into their sleeves or the palm of their hands and passed it from one to another. They talked of sheets turning red; how she'd bled so much there was no blood left. Some of them shook their heads while they stroked their bellies, swollen with babies that wouldn't soak into their beds but would birth into summer. Some of them held the children they already had; brought them from nursemaids to look at their faces, their buttermilk skin, watched their eyelashes shadow their cheeks. They passed in corridors, eyes flicking to their feet, and said nothing. Some of them let others into the room to show them where it had happened. They described the bag of soft bones, the red trickle turning into a flood, her screams, her begging face turned upwards to heaven. Some of them said it was *God's will*, or a spell from a witch and some of them still thought she was one. Some wept with empathy; some of them smirked as they blew out the candle and slept on their clean white sheets.

Solstice

On these short days we sit and tell our stories.
The clagging blackness suffocates us, stops
our voices and we stumble over details,
grasp at the truth to steady us. In the dark
I am the same as them; no different
to the chamber maid, lady-in-waiting.
We are all our own witnesses. The candle dies
and the dark fetches up our testaments:
men's hands, tongues, fingers; all the tools
of our change. Some speak of love and some
have never heard the word, never spoken it;
their lives spent feeling from one day to another.
Picking their way through the dark.

Katherine

She is gone.   But still I'm haunted
by the corners of rooms where her hair
collects   where her body   still sheds
itself   the powder she applied to her skin
floats in the air then rests in thin layers
and I touch it   smell her
I can't help myself look for her
her jewellery   is warm
with the heat of her   I turn her rings
on my fingers   hear the vows she made
feel her heartbeat in the pendant
that dips to my breasts   it's as if
she's still here   as if she's not dead.

Dropped

This time she carries low. Lit in dim twilight,
she turns her face to watch him from across
the room. He is dancing, laughing with a friend
and even from a distance she can feel his power.

He clicks; another cup is at his lips, meat
in his hand. He licks his fingers as the grease
clots on his chin. Someone joins him, curtsies
in deference and he draws a finger down her cheek.

He stands again and all around are on their feet.
He whispers something to the woman. She smiles,
lowers her eyes and walks away. He follows,
a glance across the room spared for his Queen.

We are all playing by his rule.
The epiphany comes quickly and the babe
falls in her belly to acknowledge her.
Son or daughter, it will be its father's child.

Heretic

I dream of them; their scorched, flayed flesh,
their ashy hair. The words they choke
into the suffocating air
drown out their innocence.

I am done with them; yet still they come,
crawl towards me through the flames.
My lungs are filled with acrid shame.
I breathe their godlessness.

I wake in fever, still smell smoke.
My son is brought to birth too soon,
gone, before the turn of earth.
I burn in childlessness.

Purge

Sometimes I think of you and cry.
A slow
thin
drip.

I atone in increments.
What I want
is body-heaving, weeping.
Get it over with.
Have done with it.

Jane

I marked him night after night,
my giddy odour on his face,
sticky and tart.

He took it back to her, tainted the sheets
she had stitched with their entwined initials
in the days of their new love.

How she must have hated me, held her breath
while he kissed her goodnight. Cursed me
through all her godliness and piety.

Now I'm where she was.
My replacement leaves no scent.
Her subtlety is enviable.
Her quiet name is everywhere.

Silenced

I am cast out. Marked empty and barren.
The taste of early morning, sour and dry,
holds my tongue down. I am mute.
Despite all my knowledge
and the hours of learning,

I've forgotten the sound of my own voice,
its saltwater sting, the raze of it, sore.
My throat is thick with force-fed lies.
Falsehoods fasten my lips.

Their words burn
the inside of my mouth.
I taste their acid judgment.
It blisters but still
I won't say what they want me to say.

Ya'aburnee

Arabic: 'you bury me'

Dig me down into the ground; I'll not fight it.
Cover me in leaves and dirt; let the world
have its slow vengeance.

Bury me in barren mud, red clay or fertile soil.
Let worms make homes in all my cavities,
insects dance upon me.

Bury me, I'm tired. I want to close my eyes
against another dawn, shut my ears
against your words.

Greensleeves

I have loved you so long.
Now it seems you're everywhere.
I've tried to be without you,
undone that which was written;
laws and prophesies, God-given.

You were my blood, my heart
of joy, my life's delight.
In darkest corners, sunlit courtyards,
I felt you, the whisper of you;
your skin, your deep black eyes.
And I am terrified to lose you

now, after my lips have touched
your secret places, my fingers caught
in webs I've no desire to leave.
I have been ready at your hand,
loved you for so long,

waged friends and life and land.
Wait for me in purgatory.
I'll seek the heaven of your body,
else spend eternity in Hell.
All for my lady.

Eyes

Faithless eyes watch me
through key holes.

Those who would know me,
seeing what they chose to.

This lock is all I have. A chink
through which I count the days.

My woman's body betrays me
and I am tired of pretending.

There is no sound like these footsteps,
invisible paths to end my isolation.

He has keys to name him 'gaoler',
his heft to call him 'man'.

Nothing marks my gender.
My breasts are useless here.

My womb bleeds
for the loss of me.

How to kill a butterfly

She'll come to him on the spring breeze
from her death chamber,
through corridors of men in hard black shells.

Wrapped in silk,
her mantis calling at an end,
she is the prey.

He'll have her dead in no more time
than it might take
to crush her underneath his boot.
But he'll be barefoot
and it's her neck he wants.

Her wings will beat for a second,
but in the end
she will be glad of him.

She'll be the next
in my collection, preserved
should I forget her.
The way she used to fly.

Witness

And when we spoke about it afterwards, we
all had different stories but for me
it was the quiet. The crowds were let in,
their footsteps on the stone, their yelling
to be near the front, the chomp and slurp
of beer and bread, the jostle-knock and trip
as bodies pushed against the barricade,
such as it was. Then silence as the voices faded
into something I have never heard.
And she was there, a woman unafraid
at last of what we said of her.

A good executioner

I think about you. Your little neck,
bloodless cheeks, the guilt
of your motherhood,
a small goodbye at dawn.

I was silent,
barefoot. So you
never knew which side
I took you from.
I wonder about you. His hand
on your leg, mouth watering
at the thought of you.

The way you made him wait.

Confined

They tell me to breathe.
I breathe in. My breath
is one lungful, two.

It seethes out of my nostrils,
through the gap in my teeth.
In, out. My ribcage flat,
its captive heart, slowed.

I am taller than all of them.
They scurry and fuss
at my feet. I fix my gaze
on a face in the crowd.
Keep my head up,
and breathe.

Doing things right

She likes the alchemy,
how something grown in sun
is milled and ground then risen.
How a small amount of bitterness
makes all the difference.
The way a lamb's sweet features
turn ugly, its wool shorn
then washed and spun.
How, from a language long inherited
she clothes her daughters.
She'd like to leave out punctuation
but she's learned its importance,
that leaving spaces between words
instead of commas
wouldn't suit her.

Night shift

Outside it's snowing. Nurses who have slept all day
turn from their tin of Quality Street
as you shuffle past their station to the bathroom.

A plastic jug next to your bed is filled with water you must drink,
though you want coffee because for nine months the taste
of it has made you sick and all you've drunk is tea.

The catheter tube wraps the wrong way round your leg.
It tugs inside, reminding you you're desperate to pee properly.
Your stitches pull but you still bleed like all the other mothers.

You think you can hear her from two floors down
in S.C.B.U. pick out her cry from all the others.
A tube drips your milk into her belly that will not fill.

She cries for three days until they bring her
in a Silver Cross up to the ward. You're not sure
she is yours and she still won't accept you as her mum.

T.H.O.T.
That Ho Over There

Unshackled now, their words kindle
dry ground. A pyre lit for burning.
Up from your feet to your knees singeing
80 denier Lycra. Up.
Catching the hem of the skirt
you have rolled at the waist,

to the fray of the sleeve you chew in Maths,
the heat of a bored gaze into your back. Up.
Over your chest, the prickling rash
you know will be there. Up.

Round your neck band, your face
collecting words hurled from one end
of the yard. Blood flushes through you,
from your heart, lungs full
of a thick wall of tar.

You remember how you've learned
to leave this girl who takes insults like
slag,
  whore,
    slut,
piles them up.
When enough of them gather,
they ignite and burn.

So you shake off the flames,
walk away. All that's left are ashes
where you stood. Scorch marks.
The stench of branded skin.

49

Twelfth of September 2001,
Cala Romantica, Mallorca
After Tom Weir

I should probably mention the dark.
The molasses-black hours when nobody stirred,
so quiet you could hear your neighbours cough,
turning over to reach out for each other in dreams.
Though it's not the dark you remember, but the sun
as it rose through the blue shuttered windows,
made its way through the trees, came and went
with the clouds. And Sky News was an unblinking box
on a loop in the corner of a room full of strangers;
German tourists and locals standing silent,
shaking their heads at the death toll. When they spoke
it was to us and each other, but in their own language.
No one had mobiles and the pay-phone
at the end of the road ate all your Pesetas
in a moment but your mum was a comfort
so you called every day, anyway, just to listen.
Your dreams were of being back home, but home
was a place you'd begun to lose faith in. You held on
to your kids and you prayed, because then
you still had a God you believed in.
And I should probably mention the dark.

At twenty

How hot it was that day. August tricked us
into thinking we were fine, shielding
our eyes against the sun and the future.
Things I thought would matter weren't important;
small things. A niggle, like a pebble
thrown against a window, became stuff
I couldn't say. If I'd said the words out loud
instead of wrapping them up tight
in expectations, I could have been someone
else by now. We watched the day melt.
I stopped pretending, soon after that.

Turn

Show yourself. Your face rose gold
behind the hawthorn. I can't make
my body rise; too slow, too stuck
with sadness to be anything but watcher.

I've seen the river, close to its bed
slink back, warm, a different friend
to the wildness it pretends a few months
either side of here. Midsummer moon,

if I was still the girl I used to be,
bleeding into the earth each month,
I'd see you clearer, your gentle face.
I'd know you better.

Railway child

(The Railway Children – Lionel Jeffries, 1970)

That summer was her coming of age.
Deep in green, picking rosemary,
sage at the top of the field.
Watching trains, waving at strangers.

She was everyone's favourite;
Walkabout naked. So sweet you could eat her,
and one of them tried, forgot how he'd cried
for a fatherless child

dressed in white, red underneath.
She learned pretty soon that foxes have teeth,
old men sometimes aren't nice.
Crimson always means stop.

Silent all these years

What if I were to tell you I hadn't wanted to. On nights I was too tired, mornings when I'd wanted to sleep longer. Days I ached from work or kids or homesickness. When stitches pulled, breasts leaked milk. And blood. Sometimes blood was everywhere. What if I told you some nights I was too drunk to come; I'd needed longer, that your body on mine was too heavy, mine on yours too exposed. What if I were to say that when you fell asleep I didn't and your snoring just made me resentful. What if I said *you* weren't *the one* or *you* or *you* or *you* and finding someone to feel right with would take nearly half my life. What if I were to tell you the first time wasn't that great and if I'd had the words or been able to say them, I wouldn't have said *yes*. What if I told you I didn't say *yes*. I couldn't even get up to go, or tell you what time I had to be in, or even speak to you on the phone. I stayed quiet and you never knew I hadn't wanted to. What if I were to tell you I didn't say yes.

Seen everything now

From your bedroom window
you could make out the field,
watch his slow march
from one gate to another.
And even though he was yours
for then, you knew
he was never quite with you.
You stopped watching, waiting.
You grew older, forgot him.
But still looked for him
for a long time, through
other windows. Even when
you knew it couldn't be him.
Even now, sometimes.

For whoever

I keep finding bits of you as I bring up your dead;
not knowing what they are, what they died of.
Some hold on to the bit of life they have,
don't give up easily, or else attack me
for what I'm doing; I've cursed them more than once.

I can't remember what you're called, your names
lost to moss, but I feel your cheer
in wallflowers, forget-me-nots, imposter
Spanish bluebells. I've unpicked and loosened
wind chimes from a thorn tree's branch, its music
would have once annoyed me. Now I hook it
to a lilac tree, wait for the breeze.
I wonder if you know the comfort
you'd afford me, that I'd plant handfuls
of seeds to give me hope in future.
I don't want to make this perfect – it is
better for its flaws, its crazy paths,
rotting fences and I have no need for lawns.
And it hurts, this peeling back the skin
of winter, though I feel a guilty pleasure;
glad to be exposed. I'm glad I'm home.

Home-spun

When they are toe-poked,
                arm-spurt sleeves too short.
Hemless, cotton-snagged,
        button-lost,
spun-shrunk, felted
into mat. When they are washed-grey,
darned-tight, yarn-pilled. Stitched-through
                mended.
                Handed back, pulled-out, passed on.

When she is treadle-numb, needle-sore.
           Eye-bleared from tiny pattern words,
long-awake fixing into school-good.
     Tangled, cut-down,
       un-picked
ripped-back
worn-out.

Amniocentesis

For Beattie

And when there is nothing else to do
she holds my hand. Watches with me
as the needle pierces my belly, sends in
a thin tube to suck up her cells and mine.
I have been slow to tell her, scared
of her reaction to the news of a child
there seems to be no place for. Worried
she will judge me for my carelessness.
But her words when they come
are sensible like her:
how can a baby be a bad thing?

The medium

shuffles the pack, deals on the ironing board
table in Sandra's back bedroom,

says your next child will be a boy. *The cards know*,
and when you shake your head and say it can't be,

the fortune teller says: *it's in your fate, a little boy
with curly hair.*

For a moment you smell his newborn head, kiss his nose.
Imagine him posing in photos with his sisters.

Mourn him, just the same.

Two girls
For Shamima Begum and Katherine Howard

I was a girl. Tongue-tied, almost invisible.
I hid under tables, scooped confetti
from someone else's wedding.
Until they named me, I was just a girl
with other girls in rooms, in houses,
where men came, where we lay.

We accepted compliments
which fizzed away; insults slapped.
Until my face fit someone's list
and I became a girl in a grown-up world,
where men fought men and girls
like me were sometimes in the way.

Seeing something once or twice sends cold
from your neck to your heel bone.
After that you feel nothing.

A girl is easy to forget
until she speaks, after months, years,
weeks of being silent in a place
where your face is hidden.
When you speak it's quietly and slow,
you force the words; they split the frozen air,
no one hears, so you speak louder,
and they stop the fighting
and the talking and the killing,
and turn to look.

But because you're just a girl
they hardly notice when you point out
what is happening. They don't hear
until they listen because you
have made them. Listen.

I am a girl, yet they treat me like a woman
with a woman's hair and woman's breasts
and children from my woman's womb.
And though my head thinks like a girl,
I don't have the tools to turn my thoughts
to woman's words, when I speak
they see a woman, speaking like a girl.

And then they put me out into the world.

New blood

I wept that first night, for the space
inside, for new moons passing on
without me, babies I had never wanted,
but now would never have.

Afterwards, I went home with a bag
of someone else's blood; D.N.A.
without my name. I stopped bleeding,
gave up craving Scampi Fries and ice.
I lay down in my own bed
with its crumpled sheets,
picked at stitches, ran my fingers
over a gathered seam.

Mothership

She sends blood round your body.
Round the hollowed space, scooped out
when it made you pale, ironless.

Blood rushes from organ to organ,
and you don't lose it now;
it roars in your ears at night
and when you think of your daughters.

Sleep sets you rudderless
in a body of water, and you float,
not swimming, not drowning.
You lie back, watch the moon rise.

Not Richard Gere

(Yanks – John Schlesinger, 1979)

I am wearing a dress my mother has made me
from a bolt of material off the top shelf
in a shop in Haworth. It is polka dot.

My hair is swept off my face in a roll.
My lips stained with a cherry pink lipstick
I have borrowed from my sister.

I am nineteen; Keighley station is crowded,
loud with goodbyes. I am trying not to cry.
It is 1944, you are Richard Gere and I love you.

You are not Richard Gere. It is 1984.
I am seventeen, wearing jeans.
Keighley station is silent as cease-fire. It is 1984.

You have a useless excuse.
I am watching you get on the train.
I love you. I won't see you again.

You are Richard Gere,
the train is moving out of the station.
I am waving from the footbridge.

I am nineteen.
I am wearing jeans.
You are Richard Gere.
It is 1944 and I love you.

I am seventeen.
I am waving.
I am wearing a polka dot dress.
It is 1984. I am nineteen.
I love you.
You are not Richard Gere.

Remember, blood

If you forget the pink-brown first time,
think of your surprise;
you could bleed so slowly.

If you forget the shame, think of them;
laughter as they walked away,
sit down, hide the stain.

If you forget the pain,
think how you could make yourself
come so your nerve endings hummed
and a memory from before birth
swelled and sang in your head.

If you forget your womb,
think of what it took from you,
what it gave back, ironless,
hollowed.

If you forget blood,
think how, like Mercury,
it settles, finds a shape.

How, even now it flows
through your scooped out body.

If you forget words like loss, late, missed,
think of your daughters.
One blue line, *Placenta Previa*,
Ward 14's November.

If you've forgotten how to bleed,
find a mirror, look at your face.
Remember.

The world's wife

'But there is such a strain of poetry to relieve the tragedy that the more she cries and the readers cry, the better I say.'
G. H. Lewes (George Eliot's husband), March 1860

This hair will not curl, too much of her father;
not the brains of her brother. This girl
should be seen, not heard, but she twitters,

too much fuss over butter. Little wench,
dark child, she hacks at her hair, spites her mother.
Books aren't for her; learning is men's work,

she'd do well to remember. Her place
is at home where the wheel sucks the Floss in,
spits it out again, turns days into years.

She grows uglier, hungrier. She should sit still,
content, but she runs, arms and legs,
through fields high with summer. Drifts off

with one who is meant for another; her cousin.
Comes back with her head up, no shame.
The Mill locks its doors, just herself to blame.

And now she is dead, God forgive her.
She slips without sound, her arms round her brother.
The end round these parts comes in water.

Umbilical

I feel it in private messages,
in photographs. The itch
of C-section scars, still,
the tingle of breasts,
engorged and aching.

It stretches almost to breaking
when there are miles
between us, when they
have turned their faces.
Locked me out.

They walk away and don't look
back. Returning home
when they feel the pull.

Painting-by-numbers
for H

I have never been able to draw.
At school two girls who were good at it
showed me how by following the lines
with your eyes while you make
the same marks with your pencil on paper.

My dad once helped me paint-by-numbers;
tiny spaces filled in with weird-named oils.
Forests in Alpine, ten shades of green,
the relief of blue for a mountain stream.

It was painted on plastic then shrunk
in the oven so it looked for all the world
like a miniature masterpiece.
I think he framed it.

I can't draw. But there are things I can tell you:
how you can alter the image
you have of yourself, rub out the lines,
take yourself to bits piece by piece.
Build yourself up again.

And though you look different: you are
a tango dancer in Buenos Aires,
a grandmother, long-distance swimmer,
you are still the same.

And one day there is no more paint,
no more pieces, you've filled all the spaces
with different colours. It's beautiful;
you can hardly believe you have made it.

I think you should frame it.

Fear of falling

How lovely it would be, to drop,
to feel no vertigo, but the rush of blue.
To float, like dandelion seeds blown free
from roots which tied them to their boundaries,
so they become, not weeds but ethereal
and land, as wishes, brought to whispered truth.

But how to abandon safety, an edge
so easy and so comfortable it feels like home.
To leave a crown grown tall with wisdom,
let curls fly, limbs loosen and un-stiffen
without gravity above the brown and green,
flying weightless, giddy with no fear.

How perfect, just to dive into the open
landscape, never knowing how to fall.